# Look Your Best!

## Kelly Doudna

Consulting Editor, Diane Craig, M.A./Reading Specialist

Published by ABDO Publishing Company, 4940 Viking Drive, Edina, Minnesota 55435.

Copyright © 2007 by Abdo Consulting Group, Inc. International copyrights reserved in all countries. No part of this book may be reproduced in any form without written permission from the publisher. SandCastle™ is a trademark and logo of ABDO Publishing Company.

Printed in the United States.

Credits
Edited by: Pam Price
Curriculum Coordinator: Nancy Tuminelly
Cover and Interior Design and Production: Mighty Media
Photo Credits: AbleStock, Comstock, Hemera, ShutterStock, Stockbyte

Library of Congress Cataloging-in-Publication Data

Doudna, Kelly, 1963-
   Look your best! / Kelly Doudna.
     p. cm. -- (Character concepts)
   ISBN-13: 978-1-59928-737-9
   ISBN-10: 1-59928-737-4
   1. Clothing and dress--Juvenile literature. I. Title.

GT518.D684 2007
391--dc22

                                                                    2006032294

SandCastle™ books are created by a professional team of educators, reading specialists, and content developers around five essential components—phonemic awareness, phonics, vocabulary, text comprehension, and fluency—to assist young readers as they develop reading skills and strategies and increase their general knowledge. All books are written, reviewed, and leveled for guided reading, early reading intervention, and Accelerated Reader® programs for use in shared, guided, and independent reading and writing activities to support a balanced approach to literacy instruction.

## Let Us Know

SandCastle would like to hear your stories about reading this book. What is your favorite page? Was there something hard that you needed help with? Share the ups and downs of learning to read. We want to hear from you! To get posted on the ABDO Publishing Company Web site, send us e-mail at:

**sandcastle@abdopublishing.com**

**SandCastle Level: Transitional**

# Look Your Best!

Your character is a part of who you are. It is how you act when you go somewhere. It is how you get along with other people. It is even what you do when no one is looking!

You show character by looking your best. You comb your hair. You dress properly for what you're doing. You don't go to school in your pajamas!

Miguel and Diego wear their weekend clothes because it is Saturday. On Monday, they will wear their uniforms to school. They dress properly for what they are doing.

Molly wears old clothes to sweep. She knows her new shirt is not the right thing to wear. Molly dresses properly for chores.

William dresses up for the family photo. He looks his best.

Lauren is eating dinner with her grandparents. She picks her purple dress to wear. Lauren looks her best.

Anthony loves his cow costume. He dresses properly for a costume party.

# Look Your Best!

It's Saturday morning,
and Drew is
getting dressed.
He looks in the drawer
and wonders what
would look best.

Drew is meeting
friends and wants
to look nice.
He talks with
his brother,
who gives him
some advice.

18

Drew tries on one shirt,
then tries on some more.
Pretty soon he has
tried on every shirt
in the drawer.

Drew finally picks
a shirt that's white
and yellow.
When his friends
see him, they say,
"You're a very
stylish fellow!"

# Did You Know?

School uniforms are most common in private schools. But as of 2000, one in five public schools also required school uniforms.

Until the middle of the 1800s, there was no difference between left and right shoes.

Grade-schoolers who spent their own money in 2005 on back-to-school items spent about $13 each.

# Glossary

**advice** – an opinion given about what someone should do.

**properly** – in a correct or suitable way.

**stylish** – dressed in clothes that are in fashion or that express a personal sense of style.

**uniform** – special clothes worn by all members of a group.

# About SandCastle™

A professional team of educators, reading specialists, and content developers created the SandCastle™ series to support young readers as they develop reading skills and strategies and increase their general knowledge. The SandCastle™ series has four levels that correspond to early literacy development in young children. The levels are provided to help teachers and parents select appropriate books for young readers.

**Emerging Readers**
(no flags)

**Beginning Readers**
(1 flag)

**Transitional Readers**
(2 flags)

**Fluent Readers**
(3 flags)

These levels are meant only as a guide. All levels are subject to change.

To see a complete list of SandCastle™ books and other nonfiction titles from ABDO Publishing Company, visit www.abdopublishing.com or contact us at: 4940 Viking Drive, Edina, Minnesota 55435 • 1-800-800-1312 • fax: 1-952-831-1632